YOUR KNOWLEDGE HAS VALUE

- We will publish your bachelor's and master's thesis, essays and papers

- Your own eBook and book - sold worldwide in all relevant shops

- Earn money with each sale

Upload your text at www.GRIN.com
and publish for free

Bibliographic information published by the German National Library:

The German National Library lists this publication in the National Bibliography;
detailed bibliographic data are available on the Internet at http://dnb.dnb.de .

This book is copyright material and must not be copied, reproduced, transferred,
distributed, leased, licensed or publicly performed or used in any way except as
specifically permitted in writing by the publishers, as allowed under the terms and
conditions under which it was purchased or as strictly permitted by applicable
copyright law. Any unauthorized distribution or use of this text may be a direct
infringement of the author s and publisher s rights and those responsible may be
liable in law accordingly.

Imprint:

Copyright © 2015 GRIN Verlag
Print and binding: Books on Demand GmbH, Norderstedt Germany
ISBN: 9783668744318

This book at GRIN:

https://www.grin.com/document/428437

Silvia Schilling

Christopher Marlowe's Play Edward II (1594) between Sexual and Social Transgression

GRIN Verlag

GRIN - Your knowledge has value

Since its foundation in 1998, GRIN has specialized in publishing academic texts by students, college teachers and other academics as e-book and printed book. The website www.grin.com is an ideal platform for presenting term papers, final papers, scientific essays, dissertations and specialist books.

Visit us on the internet:

http://www.grin.com/

http://www.facebook.com/grincom

http://www.twitter.com/grin_com

Table of Contents

1. Introduction..2
2. King Edward II and Gaveston..3
   2.1. Sexual Transgressions...3
   2.2. Social Transgressions..4
      2.2.1. The Distribution of Power..4

      2.2.2. The Monarch-Subject Bond..5

      2.2.3. The Image of the King..6

3. Queen Isabel and Mortimer Junior..7
4. Conclusion...9
Works Cited..10

1. Introduction

The tragedy *Edward II* by Christopher Marlowe depicts King Edward's reign, his forced abdication, and his death as well as his relationship with Gaveston and the rise and fall of his opponent Mortimer Junior.

According to the *Oxford English Dictionary*, the term transgression refers to "[t]he action of transgressing or passing beyond the bounds of legality or right; a violation of law, duty, or command; disobedience, trespass, sin."[1] In Elizabethan England, many of the acts which the *Oxford English Dictionary* defines as transgressions would have been categorized as acts of sodomy. Back then, the term sodomy "covered [...] a whole range of sexual acts, of which sexual acts between people of the same sex were only a part. It was closer, rather, to an idea like debauchery. [...] It was also a political and a religious crime." (Bray 41) Therefore, sodomy was not limited to sexual acts, but encompassed a whole range of immoral and illegal acts, much like the contemporary definition of transgression does now. This theoretical background is important to understand the use of the term in some of the cited secondary sources.

The following essay will show that the play highlights a problematic entanglement of sexual and social transgressions. It does so especially in regard to the relationship of King Edward and Gaveston, but it also interrogates the sexual and social components of Isabel's relationship with Edward's enemy Mortimer Junior. The causes and effects of the several transgressions are essential elements of the play and drive the plot forward.

At the core of the plot is the relationship between Edward and Gaveston. It is precisely the problematic entanglement of private sexual matters and public affairs seen in this relationship that leads to the other transgressions and tragic events depicted in the play. This will be illustrated through the analysis of the transgressions by Edward and Gaveston, followed by the transgressive actions of Isabel and Mortimer.

---

[1] http://www.oed.com/view/Entry/204777?redirectedFrom=transgression& (16.11.15)

2. King Edward II and Gaveston

2.1. Sexual Transgressions

The play "refuses to allow a simplistic verdict on Edward's love for Gaveston." (Stewart 93) Looking at the ideal male friendship in Elizabethan England, Edward's and Gaveston's relationship may not necessarily be of a sexual nature. It is given an ambiguous erotic undertone, which is introduced through Gaveston's ideas on how to entertain the king: "Sometime a lovely boy in Dian's shape, / [...] / And in his sportful hands an olive-tree / To hide those parts which men delight to see" (1.1.60, 63/64). While this quote certainly refers to erotic entertainment, it remains unclear if this entertainment would be of a homosexual or a heterosexual nature: "is it the body of the boy which is being hidden or of the goddess he is playing?" (Bray 49) This uncertainty can be seen as representative of the ambiguity in regard to Edward's and Gaveston's relationship and their sexuality. "Marlowe [...] places [the relationship] wholly within the incompatible conventions of Elizabethan friendship, in a tension which he never allows to be resolved" (Bray 49), leaving it open to interpretation whether or not homosexual acts are a component of this very close friendship. For the sake of this essay, I will obtain the position that the relationship is indeed a sexual relationship. Therefore, sexual transgressions in the form of adultery and homosexual acts, which Elizabethan society considered to be "a crime which anyone was capable of" (Bray 40), take place from the very beginning of the play.

Even though Elizabethan law considered sexual acts between men a crime, this offense is neither condemned nor celebrated in the play. As will be shown in detail later on, Edward's sexuality "takes on meaning primarily when [it] impinges on the political" (Thomas 2). The sexual transgressions of Edward and Gaveston are only important in relation to the social transgressions they cause, which become a threat to the just distribution of power, the monarch-subject bond, and the image of the king as natural ruler and husband.

2.2. Social Transgressions

2.2.1. The Distribution of Power

A sexual relationship between the King of England and "one so basely-born" (1.4.403) as Gaveston might be considered a breach, but would it be a relationship contained within the private sphere, it would be a nuisance the nobility would condone. This is illustrated by Mortimer Senior's statement that "[t]he mightiest kings have had their minions" (1.4.391) and the hope that "riper years will wean him from such toys" (1.4.401), suggesting that Edward's love for Gaveston might just be a phase the nobility could endure.

However, since the relationship transgresses the boundaries between private and public life resulting in favoritism concerning Gaveston, it cannot be accepted by the nobles. Edward declares Gaveston to be "Lord High Chamberlain, / Chief Secretary to the state and me, / Earl of Cornwall, King and Lord of Man" (1.1.153-155) as soon as he returns from exile to England. As Edward's brother Kent points out, "the least of these may well suffice / For one of greater birth than Gaveston" (1.5.157/8). The king also decides to give Gaveston a significant amount of wealth. Mortimer Junior states that "Gaveston hath a store of gold" (1.4.257) and "in his Tuscan cap / A jewel of more value than the crown" (1.4.414/415).

This sudden rise in power of a commoner provokes harsh reactions from Edward's closest noblemen: "Accursed Gaveston!" (1.2.4) and "villain" (1.2.11), they cry. Through these reactions, it becomes clear that the nobles condemn Gaveston and see his rise as a social transgression. Gaveston's characterization as a "villain" (1.2.11) is telling: The nobles consider his rise in power a criminal, or at least an unnatural, act, because it threatens the established social order.

2.2.2. The Monarch-Subject Bond

Another offense committed by King Edward is that he cares only for himself and Gaveston. He puts his relationship with Gaveston before the well-being of his entire realm and all the other subjects of whom he is supposed to take care. This is shown explicitly in the statements Edward makes concerning what he is willing to do to keep Gaveston at his side in England. As an example, Edward states: "And, would my crown's revenue bring him back, / I would freely give it to his enemies" (1.4.308/9), which means that Edward would be willing to give up his rightful place as king – in other words, he would abandon his people, his queen, and his kingdom – if that meant he would "have some nook or corner left / To frolic with [his] dearest Gaveston" (1.4.72/73). Edward does not seem to consider his people and his realm, all he can think about his Gaveston and his wish to never be parted from him. Mortimer Junior points out that the king "ha[s] matters of more weight to think upon" (2.2.8). He has the duty to govern and protect his people as "[t]he king of France sets foot in Normandy." (2.2.9) Edward declares this event to be a" trifle" (2.2.10) and does not concern himself further with it. Later on, Lancaster declares that "the northern borderers, seeing their houses burnt, / Their wives and children slain, run up and down / Cursing the name of [Edward] and Gaveston." (2.2.178 – 180) Similarly, "the younger Mortimer links the country's financial distress with the seductions of the favorite" (Stewart 92) by stating that "[t]he idle triumphs, masques, lascivious shows, / And prodigal gifts bestowed on Gaveston / Have drawn [Edward's] treasure dry and made [him] weak." (2.2.156 – 158)

By not exercising his responsibilities, Edward does not carry out his role of king as he should. To refer back to the definition given by the *Oxford English Dictionary*, these statements and actions are considered to be transgressions, because Edward passes beyond the bounds of what is right by violating his inherited duty and role of command. Edward's behavior therefore "both opposes and destabilizes established social and political arrangements" (Cartelli 164) as he lets his private matters affect the public life.

> To the nobility the "wanton humour" between king and Gaveston is reprehensible not because it is homoerotic: [...] there is nothing inherently subversive about the king's passion for Gaveston. However, what is subversive, as Mortimer (jr.) makes explicit, is when the king's wanton humour interferes with the discharge of his regal duties. (Thomas 4)

It is not the sexual transgression itself that causes the "unnatural revolt" (4.5.9) of the noblemen against their king and the murder of Gaveston. These actions are caused by "the overwhelmingly political implications of Edward's cultivation of Gaveston: implications that disrupt the reciprocal ties that bind king, peers and the realm." (Thomas 4). This can be seen when Lancaster urges Edward: "Learn then to rule us better, and the realm." (1.4. 39)

2.2.3. The Image of the King

The image of the king as the natural ruler by birth is threatened through his wrongdoings because the king's actions lead to his subjects calling him an "[u]nnatural king" (4.1.8/9) and one amongst "[m]isgoverned kings [who] are cause of all this wrack" (4.4.9/10). Kent warns Edward: "My lord, I see your love to Gaveston will be the ruin of the realm and you" (2.2.207/8). This is one of many examples of how "the play makes it clear that Edward's fall and eventual demise are inexorably linked to his relationship with Gaveston" (Stewart 92), putting this relationship at the root of all the transgressions found in *Edward II*.

The image of the king as a husband is also threatened. In the Renaissance, a peaceful coexistence of erotic friendships between men and marriages to women was possible (see Stewart 90), but "Edward's friendship with Gaveston is – against the grain – represented as being in direct opposition to his marriage to Isabella." (Stewart 91) When Gaveston returns to England, Isabel complains that "now [her] lord the King regards [her] not" (1.2.49) and her place at the side of the king is quickly occupied by Gaveston, which is another social transgression on his behalf. Soon, "Edward deliberately places Gaveston beside him on the throne, in the space that should be Isabella's" (Stewart 91) stating that "[i]t is our pleasure; we will have it so." (1.4.8/9) This transgression transforms Edward's private abandonment of the queen through adultery into a public abandonment and can be interpreted as "a form of sodomite misrule [which] has pre-empted right rule in the court" (Cartelli 164). After Gaveston's death, Edward's brother Kent goes as far as stating that Edward did not only put Gaveston on Isabella's throne, but on his very own throne, which would be an even greater offense. This is seen when Kent defends the murder of Gaveston and tells Edward: "Brother, in regard of thee and thy land / Did they remove that flatterer from thy throne" (3.4.10/11).

3. Queen Isabel and Mortimer Junior

The rebellion by the nobles against their king is "directed against one whom the laws protect" (Thomas 7). Therefore, even if the rebellion can be justified and is essentially caused by Edward's own transgressions, this behavior by the nobility must be called a transgression as well. The play itself stresses the fact that these rebellious actions are of the same type as Edward's own actions by linking them through the use of the same vocabulary (see Thomas 7). As an example, Kent characterizes Edward as an "unnatural king" (4.1.8), but he also condemns the rebellion as an "unnatural revolt" (4.5.9).

Mortimer Junior is the earl who takes the revolt farther than any of his peers. He does not only rebel against his king, he also conspires with the king's wife, the Queen Isabel, and enters into an affair with her. Therefore, this relationship displays an entanglement between the sexual transgression of committing adultery and the social transgression of conspiring against the king.

The sexual as well as the social breaches caused by Isabel's and Mortimer's relationship are a consequence of Edward's relationship with Gaveston. This is illustrated through Isabel's reasoning for being with Mortimer: "Isabel could live with [Mortimer] for ever. / In vain I look for love at Edward's hand [...] How Gaveston hath robbed me of his love" (2.4.60/61,

69). Thus, Isabel states that she would never be with Mortimer, had she experienced love, faithfulness, and commitment by her husband Edward.

Concerning Edward's and Gaveston's relationship, it is fairly obvious that Edward's love for Gaveston preceded the social transgressions. Gaveston's increase of power and rise in social status are a direct result of his relationship with the king. When looking at Isabel and Mortimer, the sequence of transgressions is not quite as clear. Before they conspire, it is suggested by Gaveston and Edward that they have an affair (see 1.4.147/148 and 1.4.154), but it is never resolved if this is actually the case. Their sexual relationship is only explicitly stated when Kent observes that "[...] Mortimer/ And Isabel do kiss while they conspire" (4.6.12/13), which puts the sin of adultery at the same point in time as the social crime of conspiracy, "blending eroticism with rebellion" (Shirley 285). There may have been a sexual component to their relationship before their conspiracy, but the "erotic dimension appears more clearly as Mortimer and Isabella usurp power" (Shirley 285). Just as Edward was deemed an "unnatural king" (4.1.8), he now characterizes Isabel as an "unnatural queen" (5.1.17). The play "insistently links their relationship to 'unnatural' civil rebellion" (Shirley 285), suggesting that the relationship itself can be considered an act of sodomy. Contrary to the motivation for Edward's behavior, Isabel's and Mortimer's conspiracy against the king is not caused by love for each other, but by their shared hate for Edward. The cause for their transgressions is the misdemeanor of Edward as a husband as well as a king.

By ordering the murder of the king and taking his place, Mortimer arguably commits the gravest social transgression of them all. His reign is "legitimated by no divine or lineal claim to sovereignty" (Shirely 289) and therefore a great threat to the existing social order just like Gaveston's rise was a threat. Isabel's and Mortimer's actions are just as destabilizing as Edward's and Gaveston's. "If Mortimer and Isabella inch toward sodomy by seizing power, Edward does so by disregarding it." (Shirley 286)

4. Conclusion

This essay has illustrated the transgressions concerning Edward's and Gaveston's relationship, but has also shown that this is not the only transgressive relationship depicted in *Edward II*. Edward and Gaveston are not the only characters to cross social borders, commit offenses, and threaten the established social hierarchy, but their sexual relationship is the cause of a myriad of further transgressions committed by them and other characters, especially, Queen Isabel and Mortimer Junior.

However, it has been shown that it is not the sexual relationship itself which sets the tragedy in motion. Instead, the tragedy is caused by the problematic entanglement of private pleasures and public affairs, the mix of sexual acts and politics, the indulgence in love and the negligence of one's duty in the consequence. The play provides a variety of perspectives on the topic through the myriad of characters committing wrongdoings and judging the ones of their fellow characters. It also provides the audience with many examples of what a transgression may be, such as unfulfilled duties, ignored responsibilities, adultery, ill-treatment of one's spouse, disobedience, rebellion. All of these vices are represented in the play and linked through the characters and the plot. *Edward II* does not explicitly comment or judge any of them, but interrogates their relationship through highlighting the problems themselves as well as their causes and their effects.

Works Cited

Bray, Alan. "Homosexuality and the Signs of Male Friendship in Elizabethan England." *Queering the Renaissance.* Ed. Jonathan Goldberg. Durham: Duke UP, 1994. 40-61. Web. 14 November 2015.

Cartelli, Thomas. "Edward II." *The Cambridge Companion to Christopher Marlowe.* Ed. Patrick Cheney. Cambridge: Cambridge University Press, 2004. 158-173. Print.

Marlowe, Christopher. "Edward II." *Doctor Faustus and Other Plays.* Ed. David Bevington, Eric Rasmussen. Oxford: Oxford University Press, 1995. 323 – 402. Print.

Oxford English Dictionary. Oxford: Oxford University Press, 2015. Online version: <http://www.oed.com>. 16 November 2015.

Shirley, Christopher. "Sodomy and Stage Directions in Christopher Marlowe's Edward(s) II". *Studies in English Literature 1500-1900* 54.2 (2014): 279 – 296. Web. 14 November 2015.

Stewart, Alan. "*Edward II* and Male Same-Sex Desire." *Early Modern English Drama: A Critical Companion.* Ed. Garrett A. Sullivan Jr., Patrick Cheney, and Andrew Hadfield. New York: Oxford UP, 2006. 82-95. Web. 14 November 2015.

Thomas, Arvind. "Land, Law and Desire in Marlowe's *Edward II.*" *The Marlowe Society Research Journal* 5 (2008): 1 – 8. Web. 14 November 2015.

YOUR KNOWLEDGE HAS VALUE

- We will publish your bachelor's and master's thesis, essays and papers

- Your own eBook and book - sold worldwide in all relevant shops

- Earn money with each sale

Upload your text at www.GRIN.com
and publish for free